They That Wait Upon The Lord...

William Craig Kercheval II

By: William Craig Kercheval II

Published by: William C. and Nancy M. Kercheval

Cover Artwork by: Nancy M. Kercheval (mother)

Photos by: Joanie L. Kercheval (sister-in-law)

To order additional copies of this book, contact:
Xlibris
844-714-8691
www.Xlibris.com
Orders@Xlibris.com

ISBN: Softcover   978-1-4415-9002-2
         EBook   978-1-4771-6179-1

Print information available on the last page

Rev. date: 02/24/2021

Dedication

We dedicate this book to each member of our family , and especially to Craig, for all his efforts in compiling this inspiring book of poetry.

Foreword

This book of poetry is intended to offer "hope and inspiration", as reflected in the Christian faith. It was written by our eldest son, Craig, when he was a teenager. We recently rediscovered it and decided to have it published, so that others can enjoy and be inspired by his creativity. Craig was born on January 17, 1963, in Hagerstown, MD. In 1972, our family moved to Buckeystown, MD, and to Smithsburg, MD, in 1976. Craig recently moved to Hagerstown , MD. He was always very artistic and creative, not only in his writings, but also, in his artwork and in other projects that he undertook. In his youth , he developed a very beautiful butterfly and insect collection. He especially admired the Monarch butterfly, as it is so majestic and colorful in appearance. He was an avid student of insects of all kinds and became very knowledgeable in the field. He now enjoys imparting this knowledge to his neice and nephews. To this day, when we see a Monarch Butterfly, or a Praying Mantis, we think of Craig. The butterfly symbolizes transformation to a new life and freedom, as do these poems. THUS, the cover of this book shows the Monarch butterfly, transformed from a caterpillar, to a chrysalis, and finally, to a beautiful butterfly- one of God's amazing creations. The book also shows God's handiwork in the exquisite, scenic photographs taken by Joanie L. Kercheval, Craig's sister in law; & a drawing of Christ's passionate face, done by Craig in his late teens. The cover picture of the butterfly was painted by Craig's mother, Nancy. Over the years, Craig has had several of his art works published & was the recipient of a variety of awards for his creativity in the arts. SPECIAL THANKS to Joanie for contributing her wonderful photographs to this book!

He giveth power to the faint; and to them that have
no might he increaseth strength.
Even the youths shall faint and be weary, and the
young men shall utterly fall.
But they that wait upon the Lord shall renew their
strength; they shall mount up with wings as eagles; they
shall run, and not be weary; and they shall walk, and not faint.
- Isaiah 40:29-31

No Introduction

What can be said
About one who was dead
and yet lives?
What can I say
Of One who each day
loves and forgives?
No lofty introduction
is needed for the One
See, He is the Giver
He and His Son
The tree was stiff and worn
His flesh was bruised and torn
He didn't curse one soul
Men scoffed and turned away
Still the Father's love did stay
He wanted to make us whole
No words of mine
Can this love rightly define
It's well above my mind
But every day I find
It is real.

Under His Shadow

The winds may howl
and the tempter shriek
But my soul's at rest
for it's peace I seek
It can't be found
within the earth
But only in Jesus
and a second birth
The past can be haunting
but echoes aren't real
Just set your hand to the plow
And God's power you'll feel
Don't wait for tomorrow
or another day's dawn
Believe in God's power
You're no longer sin's pawn.

I Say You Can

Doubts are stabbing
at your back
trying to throw you
off track
Makes no difference
my friend
Pain is short
it soon will end
Looks rough
But God will guide
Pretty tough
but He's by your side
the devil says
You're just a man
God offers hope
and says you can
No time for distress
It may be a mess
But the Saviour is strong
it won't be long
and I say you can.

To God Be The Glory

You gave me life
And though I died
You gave me life again
Death You defied

You teach me how
To walk with You
The more I see of You
I know You're true

You're everything
My soul desires
And when I'm caught in doubt
Your love inspires

And though I don't
Know life's full story
I say from deep within
To God be the Glory.

In My Hands

The days are long
And much is wrong
But you're in My hands

You're under attack
But don't look back
You're in My hands

The trials will cease
So rest in peace
It's in My hands

I can see all
And you won't fall
You're in My hands

Just seek My face
accept My grace
You're in My hands

My Love is true
I won't fail you
You're in My hands

You're in My heart
We're not apart
You're in My hands

It won't be long
So sing My song
You're in My hands.

Accept?

Lord
What can I say?
I am just realizing
What You have done for me
I am free
I have been so rebellious
So far out of Your plan
Yet, I am clean before You
All I did
was accept
I've just been seeing
How wayward I was
So confused
All because I turned from You
It could have been through
But, I am Your son?
Your grace is mighty!
Thank You Jesus
Help me to always walk by Your side
In Your Word I'll abide.

Get In

When you're out of God's will
How can you be sure
Of what life can offer
Given from a heart pure?

When you're trapped in confusion
And caught between lies
How can you reject something
That you've never tried

Yes, you've got to get in
And come out of the storm
And bathe in the Sonshine
His true Love is warm

So if you walk in darkness
Don't criticize light
Come on out of your tomb
Your joy is His delight.

I've Been Waiting

I've been waiting
for you to make your choice
I've been calling
though you deny my voice

My arms are reaching
Come children, unto me
My Love's unceasing
Accept it and be free

You have been running
Too long from the unknown
But if you'll listen
All truth will be shown

You have been seeking
Deep inside you have a quest
You may be doubting
Just put me to the test

I know it's empty
Though you have gained it all
Your foes are waiting
for the day you trip and fall

Still I've been waiting
Far above your pains and fears
Your eyes are yearning
to release a thousand tears

Time's growing shorter
You must not be deceived
I'm right beside you
waiting to be received

The hour's ripe now
Let Me in and you will see
You are in bondage
But I died to set you free

Let Go

He gave
the gift
Accept
relax
Let go

He gave
His life
on
a tree
long ago

You can't
repay Him
just
rejoice
with glee

Don't try
to grasp
it
Praise Him
and
Be free.

Come As A Child

Come as a child
Don't delay
Receive His grace today

Tell Him you're sorry
He'll forgive
And commit unto Him your way

A child's faith
is all it takes
All who ask receive

Jesus' just
a prayer away
Accept Him and believe.

A Friend

A friend is one
whose always there
To lift a burden
And show they care

A friend would never
let you down
Though in your tears
You nearly drown

A friend would always
Pick you up
And when you're thirsty
Fill your cup
,
A friend would give
Up his own life
To put an end
To all your strife

I have a friend
Who's just this way
His name is Jesus
I'm His to stay!

Something Better

There's something better
In the air
I think that you
can feel it

There's something better
waiting there
No enemy
can steal it

It's Jesus Christ
The Son of God
He's knocking at
your heart

Just let Him in
And on you'll trod
On a road
To God's own heart.

Come On Now

The road is narrow
that is true
But our journey's
almost through

I know you're wounded
But I will heal
And soon your doubts
I'll surely steal

Come on, now, child
Not much farther yet to go
I hold you safe
Though cold winds blow

Just a few more steps
don't quit now
We're going to arrive
Though you don't know how

No need to struggle
The battle's mine
Come on, now, child
You're doing fine.

Greater

Do you see God
with a doubt?
He's greater

Do you see Him
with a stain?
He's greater

Do you grasp Him
in your mind?
He's greater

No matter how
You see Him now
He's greater!

Lean On Me

Weary one
You walk slowly
But lean on me
I too am lowly

It's true that I
am God's own Son
And upon a cross
The victory I won

But don't you know
I am not proud
Though angels voice
Their praise aloud

Come
Lean on Me
I'll bring you rest
When trials come
They're just a test

But weary one
My yoke is light
Lean on Me
and walk upright.

Be Free

Don't hang on
Let go
Be free my son
To grow

What's in that pride
or vision you hold?
Only My way is truth
It can't be sold

But I bought you
Wasn't too long
From the day I hung
upon that cross
Sing My song

I know of the deceit
So many lies on the path
But come and seek Me
They'll be consumed by
My wrath

Your mind can't understand
But I speak to your soul
I only want you to be free
Give me control
You'll see.

I'm Sorry

You have
been good to me
Guided
and cared for me

I have
done wrong to you
cursed
and distrusted You

Now I'm
so sorry
For I see you've planned well

Now I'm
So sorry
I've just got to tell
Lord You've seen me through
Our love sure grew

You have
listened and talked to me
Provided
and prepared for me

I have
backed away from You
run off
and fled from You

Serve Him

Come forth
Serve the Lord
no man does He
cast out

You cannot
serve two masters
Of this
there is no doubt

Come follow
Christ is faithful
the Good Shepherd
you can trust

Ever loving
He will keep you
Even as
time turns to dust.

Now I'm
Just sorry
I didn't trust You all the way

Now I'm
so sorry
This had to be the way
But Lord You've seen me
through
Our love's as good as new.

Victory

Victory
true victory
leaves nothing to be desired
Contains no trace
of despair
Nor the faintest hint
of doubt
And when it is come
It does not end
But is as eternal as Hope
And as timeless as Love
It can never be stained
By darkness
Or understood
By logic
Neither can the mind
Perceive it's infiniteness
Nor the eye
The excellence of its beauty
Yet simple faith
Can tap its glory
If we turn from defeat
And through the blood of Christ Jesus
Seek the face of God.

Road to Recovery

Been away so long
From love's sweet song
I know I've lost my way

But now I know
Our love will grow
I'll walk with you every day

I've hurt and I've cried
But to sin I've not died
Yeah, I'm looking to the Son

And the past is only yesterday
When I think of You all I can say
is You're the One

Road to Recovery
I know I'm free
On my road to recovery
It's love I see.

The Way, the Truth, the Life

Are you confused
Is little clear
Do thoughts of dying
Bring you fear?

Listen friend
I once was there
And life was something
hard to bear

Many tried
To point the way
But only one
Had truth to say

They all had theories
But none were true
For after death
They'd fall right through

His name was Jesus
The Son of God
Now on His paths
I humbly trod

Yet one man gave
More than the others
He gave us truth
And called us brothers

He's set me free
And promised more
In His home in heaven
So much love in store

And more than that
He gave His life
So sin no longer
would bring strife

Just let Him in
Your search will cease
Come follow Him
and find your peace.

The Battle Cry

It was impossible
the odds were too great
Death, sin and misery
seemed to be the only fate

The enemy's time was short
but his wounds took their toll
and it appeared
he soon would take control

Then a light came down
that shined brighter than defeat
It seemed hope was revived
and though weak we weren't
yet beat

But then the light went out
Storm clouds gathered on the
scene
Darkness was evident
for not a single face could beam

Yet as I looked in awe
The light looked up and
cried
"Father forgive them"
then He bowed His head and
died

The tomb was dark and cold
everything was lost
But still we had to win
no matter what the cost

The stone was rolled away
The light had returned
One thing was different
though
So much brighter it burned!

Now the enemy
must bury all their dead
Under the King we're
marching
I see victory just ahead.

You've Blessed Me

Deep
within my heart
there's a treasure
that you're slowly
revealing to me

Lord, so deep
within my soul
Hope without measure
but I must remain lowly
for others to see

Father
Father
You have blessed me
It's not my own doing
You've just blessed me
satan's tried
to destroy
but I'm not just a toy
for in You
is my life and song.

My One Regret

Lord,
the trials have come
but soon they'll flee

Lord,
I used to run
but You caught up with me

Now,
my one regret
is that I've just one life
to live

Oh Father,
to You and in Your name
all that I have, I give.

It's Too Late

It's over now
the memory
No more darkened skies
My eyes can see

You went too far
You took the blame
There is no turning back
I'm not the same

You paid the price
You broke my chains
You wiped the tears away
You stole my pains

Yes, it's too late
We're going to win
Over death and misery
Over fears and sin

No turning back
My heart's on fire
I've looked sin in the eye
and called it a liar

It's too late now
the victory's won
All praise and glory be
To God's only Son

He died for you
He died for me
Nothing can bind us now
Can't you see we're free?

Just praise His name
Just lift Him up
He'll comfort you
and fill your empty cup

It's too late now
The night is past
Christ's love has conquered all
The day will last.

On That Day

I bathed in the light
of my Father's throne
I was sent down to earth
To finish my growing

It was pure joy at first
Received a warm reception
Then came the trials
fears and deception

I really lost my way
But Jesus reached down His hand
I was weak when I called Him
Now I can firmly stand

He had quite a bit to work out
But took on the situation
I don't know how He did it
But I love His consolation

Someday, face to face, I'll meet Him
And that day's not far away
Soon, face to face, I'll greet Him
today could be the day

And on that day
I'll forget my misery
Yes, I'll even
lose the memory
The strength I gained
will still be there
But without a pain
or worldly care
Yes, on that day
The victory will be won.

I Remember

I remember,
the joy
the glow
The trusting heart
the love
the peace
The hope of Spring
the butterflies
so close, so far
The old song I could sing

I remember,
the pain
the doubts
The broken heart
the hate
the anxiety
The troubled soul
the sin
the fear
The words that took their toll

I remember,
the hope
the warmth
The words of truth
His joy
His peace
The cross He bore
the nails
the blood
The Love I still adore.

Your Turn

I'm so weak
and weary
The sky is blue
But I can't see clearly
I may be selfish
and self-centered, that's
true

But Lord,
Right now I put my trust
In You
I can give no more
My hand is sore

Life seems old
My heart is so cold
I once knew love
But I have fallen
Take my tiny hand
and heed my calling
My life is yours for the
taking
Yeah, I'm yours for the
breaking
Then You can start remaking
my life.

Teach Me Now

Now that I'm new
Help me see You
Teach me the ways
of Your heart

Now that I'm free
Keep Your hand upon me
So we'll never again
be apart

I know I crawl slow
On the path I should go
But I'm only a babe
after all

The old ways are dead
Now by You I am led
Hold on to me, Lord
'for I fall.

With Love

I know you don't understand
But you can trust me
The road is rough sometimes
I know
But I am with you

It's hard to see down there
From where you are
But I will be your eyes
I hear your prayers
I save your tears

You know it didn't start this
way
It was much better
But be patient
I will fix things
I already have

You can't see me yet
You're not ready
But you will be
Together we will share eternity
I only want the best for you

That's why I'm cursed by some
They can't accept my eternal
plans
which are perfect and complete
They want it all in a day
But I still call them

Wait on me
My Son has been waiting
patiently for you
He Loves you very much
Even as I Love Him
My Spirit will comfort you

It's almost over now
as you can see
Your mansion is complete
But you must take up your cross

And soon you can exchange it
for a crown
please trust me
I will never forsake you
With Love,
Your Heavenly Father

Where Is Your Sting?

Where is your sting
now that you're in hell?
Where are your lies
now that you're in a cell?

Where did your plans go
to rule o'er the earth?
Now that Christ has given
to us a new birth?

Yes, you've lost it all now
you lost it back then
When you stepped out of place
and tried to fool men

But you didn't make it
and now it's you that's dead
And we're getting stronger
On Christ's Love we are fed

You'll have to think back now
and forever more
Of the Love you let slip by
that makes you so sore

No, you didn't win it
And you never will
For the true Love of Jesus
Lives in our hearts still!

The Caterpillar

Little caterpillar
what is your secret?
How can you proceed
Unaware of your fate
Moving through the foliage
Nibbling what is before you
Without a care

I'm sure somewhere within
Lies the image of your true face
But do you know?
So contently you crawl
Through the jungles of life
Leaving old ways behind
To be carried away on the wind

And how blessed the day
When your rest is found
in a cocoon of peace
Unaware of the blizzard without
Only dreams of what is next
to delight you

Winter fades away
Suddenly - your time is come!
With renewed joy you gather up
your strength
And on wings of glory
ride the warm winds of Spring

Christmas

Christmas is a day of Love
a gift of hope sent from above
It wasn't asked for, but it came
and Jesus Christ
was its sweet name
And on that day a star shone bright
and wise men came
to see the sight
in a manger on the straw
the Son of God is what they saw
as they looked into
His bright young eyes
they didn't know He'd someday die
upon a cross
at Calvary
shamed and bleeding
for all to see

men would reject Him
and couldn't know
what was concealed
behind His glow
and yes
He knew it
as He lay
upon the comfort
of the hay
that He would die
what men would say
He even knew
of you and me
Yes, He was God
He could foresee
but even knowing
of His fate
His smile shone bright
For His Love
Was GREAT!

Keep Walkin'

The dawn is near
no need to fear
Keep walkin'

His Love is strong
You won't go wrong
Just keep walkin'

He loves you all
and you won't fall
If you keep walkin'

Don't look behind
or pain you'll find
So keep walkin'

He'll hold your hand
If you'll just stand
and keep walkin'

We're family
and victory
is just a step away
Don't hesitate
joy is our fate
today could be the day

So keep walkin'
He said we'd win
Now keep walkin'

He conquered sin
Just keep walkin'
Hold up your chin and
keep walkin'

That's what I'll sing
Keep walkin'
Christ is King
So keep walkin'.

Don't Believe A Liar

A fire is burning
Far away from God's glow
A lake of fire and flames
Where pain only can grow

It was never intended
for one man on the earth
Since Christ Jesus offered
to all a new birth

No, don't you
Believe a liar
Whose doom is in the lake of
Fire
No, don't you
Hop aboard the trip of pride
Many have tried, and in the
end died

The God of love is pained
At the evil one's fate
He was the splendor of heaven
He looked pretty great

But you see he slipped
into a lie from within
Pride is so parasitic
and so foolish a sin

He could have repented
from the deed he had done
But he fell ever farther
From the Father and Son

Now it's just too late
The decision is past
When his fiery end comes
It will eternally last

So don't you
Ever believe in a liar
His soul is dark
and blind to love's fire
Now come along
and sing the Lord's song
When our trust is in Jesus
There 's no way to go wrong.

Hidden In Thee

Hidden in Thee
Now I am
So free
Clean again
I see

You did it
Through Jesus
By Your grace
Spotless now
and in place.

Thanks

Thank You, Jesus
What more can I say?
Thank You, Father
You've brought back the day

I don't understand You
But I am humbled
So carelessly I've stumbled
Thanks.

You Rescued Me

Reflecting back
To days of old
I see how Your Love
has guided me

I rebelled
at first
So confused about my identity
You perservered

Dear Father
You rescued me
And continue to hold me
safely and tight.

Fear

It's impossible to know
the meaning of God's love
without first knowing fear

You can never grow
If you seek deceiving
shortcuts
And fail to hold His law
dear

Knowing from experience
I see fear is the start
Of an everlasting Love with
God

Learn fear and obedience
Don't stray from the narrow
path
Trust the Lord and in joy
you'll trod.

Pride

Pride tries
to work its way in
Like a self-righteous cancer
the first and worst sin

I know Lord,
These poems came from You
Yet as I wrote
outside the pride grew

But Lord,
You are within me
though pride tries
so consistently

I know that You
Are far greater than a lie
That's why right now
I tell pride goodbye!

Forgive Me

Maybe I said something
You didn't like
And You just told me
To take a hike

I might have wounded You
quite possibly
Maybe I hurt You deep,
deeper than I see

Or, am I the one
who cruelly spoke
and maybe Your confidence
I broke

I'm so sorry now
Can't you see?
I'd cry for You
Please forgive me and be
free.

Nothing Less

Nothing less
than the truth for me
and that goes for
eternity

I won't bow down
to a lie
God offers true Love
I won 't be shy

Brother or sister,
Are there lies on your
path
Give them up to the Lord
Let them bow to God's
wrath.

Did You Ever?

Did you ever
See an artist
Paint a portrait so gently
He forgot to look at his model?

Did you ever
See a musician
Concentrating so intently
He forgot to read the music?

Did you ever
See a movie
So alive and realistic
It didn't need film?

Did you ever
See a Christian
So strict and legalistic
He forgot how to love?

Did you ever
Judge another
So harshly and cruel
You forgot Christ forgave you?

Just remember
He's your brother
Did you ever take the time
To pick him up?

I'm Thirsty, Lord

Been so long
Since I took a drink
Life seems complex
It's. hard to think

I need Your peace
I have Your hope
But it seems like I'm slipping
down the slope

So thirsty, Lord
Been a long time
I need Your Spirit
To make life rhyme

I won't forget
The way it felt
When beside my bed
I humbly knelt

I opened the door
and asked You in
I knew Your peace
was free from sin

But Lord,
Can't hold out much longer
Need a drink of Your Love
To make me stronger

I'm not saying
You've done me wrong
But I just want
To sing joy's song again.

The Sword Of The Spirit

When doubts and dares
Stand in your way
Don't let them move you
On truths' path stay

The trials will come
To make you strong
For it is to Me
that you belong

My Love is true
And hard to see
But all will be clear
When you are free

The road is rough
But you need not fear it
For when danger threatens
Swing the sword of the
Spirit.

Resist

Resist the devil
And he will flee
While you march on
In victory

When you're tempted
Just say NO!
On truths' path
you will go

Freedom will come
to you someday
Resist death's lies
don't go astray

It will be worth it
In the end
stand firm in Christ
don't bend.

Your Way

My way sees me
It's not free
It's distorted
I see

So Lord, show me
I know I've slipped
Forgive me if I'm vain
In Your hand I'm gripped

I question You
as if You were a child
Forgive me, Father
If Your wisdom I've defiled

I don't know what
You're going to do
But just do it Your way
I'm trusting You.

If You Love Me

You can accept
My gift of life
But if you love Me
don't live in strife

I gave to you
My only Son
And words of truth
To make us one

Oh I love you,
And want you to be free
But keep My word
If you love Me.

I Can't

So late at night
You want me to write
But I can't

I'd like to proceed
totally freed
But I can't

I'd just like the thrill
of jumping doubts hill
But I can't

Yet one fact keeps me sane
Though through trials I'm so vain
You can!

Always

Always hope
along the way
Always Love
to pass the day
When I'm with You

Always freedom
when I'm bound
Always peace
There to be found
when trials are through

Always joy
to everlast
Always spring
when Winter's past
and snowfalls cease

Always strength
To pass the test
Always sleep
When I need rest
Soon full release.

Hope

In the heat of the battle
When no end is in sight
As our hopes start to fade
Into the dark night

Though nothing appears
To be in the right place
And of love, joy, and peace
There isn't a trace

I can still hear God's voice
faintly as it may sound
urging me to proceed
Now in hope I abound.

Rest In Peace

The war was fought
Your soul was bought
Now evil's locked in hell

The trials came
I'm still the same
No more will death rebel

The arrows soared
The lion roared
But old ways now depart

The Spring is here
No need to fear
You're safe within My heart.

Marching On

On we go
on we climb
No time
to look behind

We've given all
We're marching on
Getting closer
to the Son

Hear His voice
calling me
To come home
And be free

Hear His song
Though we're so
far away
But on we march
On we climb
All we need
He will provide
I can see
Every doubt
just slip away

Oh I see
His blessed face
shining from
the hill above
How I long
to rest in His strong
arms
Yes I know
That my mansion
is just a step ahead
and His peace
just a stepping stone
away
Some have strayed
far behind
But He's rescued every-
one
and I know
Not much farther now
to go.

At Last

I loved you My son
Before you were born
I loved you before you could see
I wanted to touch you
But I knew what was best
For this blessed day I could foresee

I knew you were confused
And that your heart was troubled
You couldn't see this far ahead
But you've trusted in My name
And no longer seek sin's way
You've carried My old cross instead

Don't you see I have waited
So long for you child
And at last I can show you
My face
You have overcome
Through the blood of My Son
And through faith have
accepted My grace

Now at last I can show you
The "whys and the hows"
Now at last I see you understand
That t'was all done in true Love
and all for the best
So you wouldn't die in
sinking sand

No more will you cry
No more will you question
Yes, the mystery of My Love is past
My glory's revealed
And in My Love you're sealed
We can walk hand-in-hand now

My Hero

My Hero's far apart
But in my heart
He died for me
Now I can see
He fights for me
Constantly
He promised eternal life
without strife
He does not age
and builds me in His image
My Hero will not fail
He took the nail
I know He will win
He did over sin
Only His eyes have sight
In His great Love is might
I can't see Him yet
But I'll never forget
The price for my soul
Now He has control
My Hero is my creator
No one is greater
I am His also

A Glimpse Of God

I caught a glimpse
of God today
In the sunset
Far away

I heard His voice
As a sparrow sang
And as night
burst into day

I saw Him there
among some clouds
Though His image
was not clear

I felt Him stir
within my heart
I had
To shed a tear.

Everything But Up

You give me life
and air to breathe
You give me ears and eyes
and touch to perceive
You give me warmth
and winter snow
You give me power
When I am low
Your word is a sword
that divides at the core
Your Spirit is infinite
There is always more
Your faithfulness
is like Noah's rainbow
You make a way
When there's no place to go
You give your best
You fill my cup
You give me everything but up.

His Love

Why did He die
You want to know
Was it just for fame
was it just for show?

Or just another
Thing to do
To pass the time
as conflicts grew?

Perhaps you even
turn aside
the thought the Son of God
had died

Upon a tree
Age thirty-three
For the simple cause
Of you and me

Well one thing's true
His word remains
Whether you believe
of the cross's blood stains

And another thing
You must inquire
Before you call
This man a liar

Is how He ever
kept His love
His quiet peace
white as a dove

As he hung there
In His pain
That love
That true love
stayed the same

For He didn't curse us
Or end our lives
"Forgive them Father!"
Is what He cried

Now I don't know
What's in your heart
Or if you see life
In the dark

But one thing's sure
From what I see
That the love of Jesus
Is for me

You can reject Him
It's up to you
But just remember
His love is true.

In Return

I gave you life
you died to sin
I sent my Son
so you could live again
Now in return
all that I ask
is not a sacrifice
or holy task
I seek your heart
I want your lives
Man can't find peace alone
No matter how hard he strives
So come to me
I'll see you through
and give your heart's
desires
freely to you
Don't try to hide
or run away
My love's eternal
I'm here, today.

For Your Glory

I don't know why
you chose me
Or my family
I don't know how
You'll use me
Or tomorrow where I'll be
I just know that
You've done it all
For the purpose of Your
Glory
And I thank You for
Your saving grace
that ended sin's dark
story.

Yet

I was chained
Yet
You freed me

I am weak
Yet
You keep me

I fall often
Yet
You pick me up

I'm stubborn
Yet
You don't give up.

In The Night

So hard to see
Lord, I feel so lost
I need to feel Your love
No matter what the cost

Oh Lord, I
Am just burning to cry
If you don't reach down soon
I'm going to die

Oh Lord, its cold
And my heart's not too bold
But You can change a life
Or so I am told

In the night
When the fight
is at hand
I feel I'm sinking
sinking deep in sin's sand

But Lord,
You hold the full deck
Reach down Your loving hand
and save my neck.

Everything

He gave me
my first breath
He put in me
a dream

I was too young
to realize
that He alone
was life and truth

But you know
He held on anyway
Now I see
the gift of life is free
All that we can hope to do
is live each day for His
glory

Everything
He gave
Our lives
He died to save
He gave me everything
Before I knew
Oh, all I can say
Is thank You.

Come To Me

There's no place left
to hide your pain
Unless you lay it down
it will remain
Do not look back
the past is gone
Take a step towards me
and sing my song
I'll take your hand
and guide the way
Just come to me
find peace today.

One Step At A Time

From behind the crib's prison bars
every step looks a step too far
Father's voice calls you closer
though its like reaching a star
Then one day the foot responds
and in one accord you proceed .
The crib looks barren now
You are freed.

This Family

Lord, how could I deserve
That family I did not reserve?
Must have been Your love
Lord, sometimes I take them for granted
But I pray I've also planted
Some of Your love
This family of mine
Is truly a treasure divine
Given from above!

Home

My heart is longing
for the place I've been belonging
Since I met Jesus

My soul is burning
For I'll soon be returning
to my place in glory

I pray I've helped someone
through the love of God's own Son
to join me in paradise

Can't deny I want to leave
But I pray you'll too receive
the gift of eternal life.

Little Children

Little children
Beware
Of the trap
and the snare
that await
on the highway of life

Little children
stand tall
On God's word
you won't fall
Though others
will choose sin's dark strife

I was just
where you are
Hadn't gone
Very far
And I slipped
in the quicksand of sin

But Christ
picked me up
put joy back
in life's cup
And I've learned
Not to follow bad men

Put your trust
in the Lord
and you'll stay
in accord
If you'll simply trust
and obey

Accept Him in
to your heart
He won't ever
depart
And safe in His love
you will stay.

Free Indeed

The chains to sin
were tight and firm
All I could really do
was moan and squirm
I was in bad shape
As far as I could see
There was no escape
Then I met someone
Not just anyone
He's that guy they nailed to a tree
Said He was God's own Son
But then many doubted
"Crucify Him!", they shouted

But this person I know
Conquered the tomb
He made a place for me in glory
Where there's plenty of room
Now I can see
Past all my misery
Some may scoff
But one thing I know
I'm a free man
Though it started out slow
I found the key
Jesus set me free.

Your Quest

You wake
And you sleep
But what is it you seek
A day's pay
or the praise of your peers?

Days come
and go
Some fast and some slow
As months
pile up into years

Long ago
Life was new
Nothing seemed to stop you
From singing
In the midst of all strife

But as
You proceed
Without someone to lead
The truth
stabs at you like a knife

Something's not
in its place
In the flow of life's race
Could it be
You left something behind?

Remember
the love
Peaceful as a dove
in your heart
that was not of the mind?

As a child
You were free
But now you can't see
that the glow
you had then was for real

But you know
Jesus died
So in peace you'd abide
far away
from the pain that you feel

He knows
It's been rough
And your true heart got tough
as sin's sting
blinded you with its charms

But His Love
Hasn't died
And He calls you to hide
Once again
Safe in His loving arms.

Serve The King

So short
Don't you know that sin's sport
is so short
You lay in defeat under
Satan's seat
you give him all and he kills you

So long
When you serve the Lord
So long
Joy and peace you can't afford to let go
He gives you more
than He takes

Serve Him
His yoke is light
You can serve Him
No need to fight
Give in
the time is right
You can resist and remain uptight
But He cares
and He wants you to be free.

Hit And Run

The devil teases
but never pleases
He'll give you all
just to watch you fall
But God takes care
of His own
They sometimes suffer
but are never alone
Jesus loves them
with all His heart
His eye's upon them
though they are apart
They need not worry
though in the heat of their
pain
Jesus soon
will send the Spirit's rain

Hit and run
that's the devil's game
fame and fun
it always ends the same
Get out!
Now don't you know
that Jesus' arms
are reaching out to you
You can turn away
But His love will stay
For you see
He's real and true
Now take a step to His Love
It's closer than miles above
Open your heart to His
gentle touch
He loves you so much .

Author Unknown

He wrote the story
The story was love
He stepped in Himself
gave his Son from above

He offered new life
Sight for the blind
Yet most turned their backs
and left Him behind

His love was so true
That He died on a tree
All that He wanted
was for us to be free

But many scoffed
At the love He had shown
discarding His truth
as if Author unknown.

A Tear For You

A tear for You
oh pure in heart
So misunderstood

A tear for You
oh true in deed
Few see that you're good

A tear for You
Dear heavenly Father
Like the ones you shed for me

A tear for You
Sweet Lord of Love
When will our blind eyes see?

Don't Stop Investing

Some hearts are stubborn, others rough and worn
Some have long been bleeding, battered, bruised and torn
But keep on sowing God's love
Its supply will not go dry
You may get hurt for trying
and find you, yourself, will cry
But don't stop investing
plant the seed with warmth and care
Make sure it is supplied with Sonshine
Moisture and the proper air
It won't take long before you see
Its power flowing back to you
Yes, keep on planting God's Love
It's alive and always true.

Share

Recognize
your brother's worth
Accept his kindness
And give to him
what you can give
In Christ's Spirit you must live

Look in his eyes
see a portion of Me
Listen to his words
Do unto him
As you would for yourself
Don't put him on the shelf

Above the skies
I watch you
Don't make Me cry
My Son gave all
when He was there
So accept My Love, and share.

Printed in the United States
By Bookmasters